God is just a comedian
we are afraid to laugh at.
—attributed to Voltaire

I laughed
and laughed
and laughed
and laughed
and laughed.
—attributed to Charles Bragg

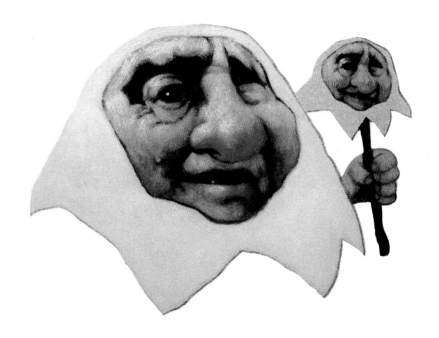

The Absurd World
of
Charles Bragg

Text
by
Geoffrey Taylor

Arcade  PUBLISHING
New York
Little, Brown and Company

Page 1: *The Blessed Father.* Etching
      Pan. Oil, 8 x 6″

Pages 2-3: *The Asylum*, 1968. Oil, 16 x 34″.
      Collection Gallerie Coté,
      Rockville Centre, Long Island

Page 4: Untitled. Pencil

Title page: *Jester.* Oil
      Untitled. Oil on wood

Right: *Self-Portrait with Models*.
      Lithograph, 9½ x 17″

Revised Edition

Special photography on pages 13, 14, 29, 36
courtesy David Cieslikowski and Joyce Gold
The Spirit, page 21, courtesy San Francisco Academy of Comic Art

Library of Congress Cataloging-in-Publication Data
Bragg, Charles.
  The absurd world of Charles Bragg / text by Geoffrey Taylor. —
Rev. ed.
    p.   cm.
  ISBN 1-55970-130-7 (HC)
  ISBN 1-55970-129-3 (PB)
  1. American wit and humor, Pictorial.   I. Taylor, Geoffrey,
1950–   II. Title.
NC1429.B733A4 1991
741.5′092 — dc20   90-20240

Published in the United States by Arcade Publishing, Inc.,
New York, a Little, Brown company

HC: 10 9 8 7 6 5 4 3 2 1
PB : 10 9 8 7 6 5 4 3 2 1

Published simultaneously in Canada by Little, Brown & Company
(Canada) Limited

Printed in Japan

And He Saw That It Was Good, 1972. Oil, 10 x 14″. Collection Peter Marshall

Ship of Fools,
1974.
Oil, 28 x 22″.
Collection
Mr. and Mrs.
Robert Collins,
Palos Verdes,
California

*Lord of Earthly
Delights*, 1980.
Oil, 18 x 16″

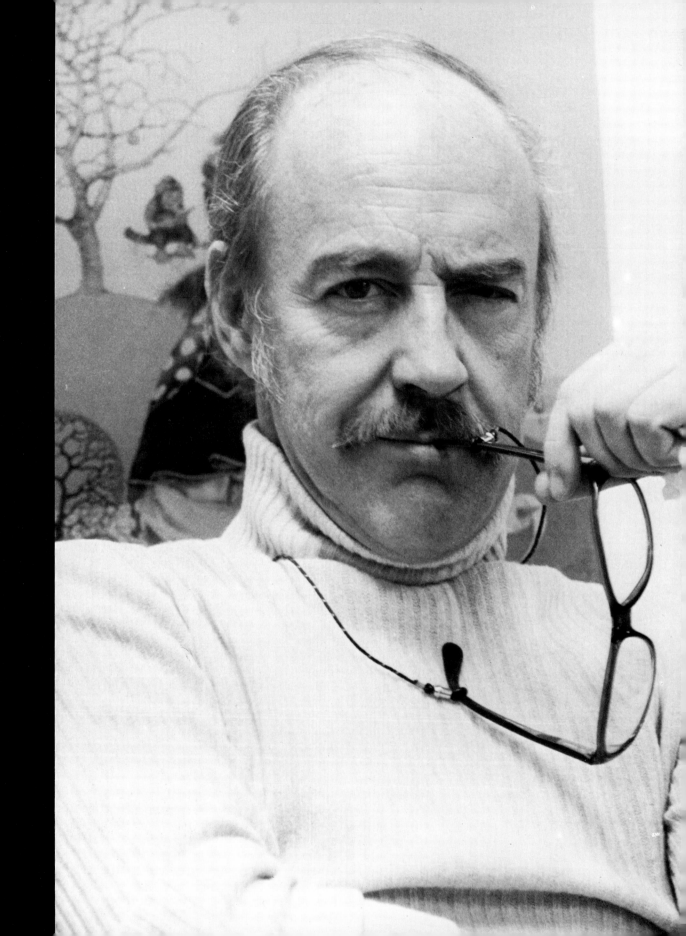

Travels with Charlie

The seat of power

You have been watching Bragg all afternoon. He is consolidated in a back corner of his studio and sits in a simple black chair that is pulled up to a plain wooden desk. He bends over his etching plate obsessively pulling little lines out of his imagination and placing them on the raw zinc with a meticulous fury.

There is a distinctive scotch-taped quality to his workspace. Yellowed notes and forgotten reminders dot the walls. A map of the world hangs to one side. Next to him sits an often-used file cabinet stuffed full of pictures and clippings; the drawers have labels such as "punims" and "circus" and "war." And dangling from a random nail, a hand grenade looks ready—no doubt Bragg's last-ditch defense against the lunatic fringe outside.

His arsenal

Moments seem long and awkward to you as Bragg works silently to the strains of Mozart's *Jupiter Symphony*. The two artists move with a singular harmony. Wolfgang runs his progressions while Charlie syncopates with slices and arcs and staccato dots across the plate. You feel like an intruder. Even more so if he stops to cast an eye your way; it is a suspicious look that picks you clean . . . your mismatched socks, that smudge on your rumpled shirt, bypassed orthodontia, unwanted hairs—unwanted moments such as these. Your spirits sink as you realize that you may find your collective foolishness immortalized at some later date. Caught as you are, you can only give your best idiot's grin.

Bragg rarely speaks, a fact that only amplifies the subtle but pervasive cacophony of the place. There is the needle's scratch. And outside, the daily Beverly Hills street rumble. An electric fan. A ringing phone. This dull hum of civilization appears to be what Bragg thrives on. It is the masses in motion. The rhythm of life in the eighties.

If Charlie's attention does wander at all, it's usually only to gather more material— to rummage through his clipping file or gaze out his window. You watch as he raises his binoculars to his eyes to pull into sharp focus another piece of human wonderment on the street below. That studio window provides a box seat for the passing human parade, and Bragg rarely misses a performance. As he finds his mark, he

A look that picks you clean

13

Bragg's box seat

The Human Race. (detail from
The Asylum)

Painful empathy. *(Objection Sustained)*

shakes his head as if amazed. "The human race. It's everywhere." You note a whimsy in his inflection—a mischievous animation that grabs you and makes you wait and hope for more.

But to no avail, for he is already back at his etching plate. Back in his artist's haze where those little lines become the grizzled and gnarled and puckish and pompous and, well, human faces that explain Bragg's point exactly. For there, in his studio, staring out from every wall, the myriad little Braggian eyes peer down at you.

It is the human race.

It is everywhere.

Charles Bragg is a devoted student of the human race. As one of the master observers of contemporary times, he and his little figures have etched their way into the American heart. His is a unique perspective on the human comedy—it is the reassuring viewpoint of the fellow traveler. If you recognize yourself in a pained expression on one of his character's faces—a look so precisely rendered that your empathy is spontaneous and unconscious—it is because Bragg has been to the mountain and suffered that bit of tangled reality himself. He is the constant observer, but never the innocent bystander.

In fact, away from the concerns of his work and his studio, Charlie is something of the grand celebrant of life and its follies. The Bragg known to his wide circle of friends and fans is nothing like the distracted artist who works silently in his studio. Rather, the real Bragg is a hopelessly social beast—relaxed, articulate, playful, and...very, very funny. His quick-witted commentary is endlessly surprising. Heretical and irreverent, he has the verbal pace and timing of a comic master. His facial expressions move across the same emotional range you see in his little people: anguish, embarrassment, lechery, and incredulity are all feigned with equal conviction and charm. He clearly gets a kick out of being paid to keep us laughing.

That wit as revealed in his work is the element which is distinctly Bragg's. He creates from the heart and laughs a bit all the while. Be it a broad-nosed alderman or a penitent parishioner, Charlie's figures look out at the world with sad-eyed resignation. They may show abandonment, but never bitterness. The mark of Bragg's affirmative ironic whimsy is unmistakable. "I've been described as a combination Charles Schulz and Hieronymus Bosch... I have the technical skill of

Schulz and the sense of humor of Bosch." His self-deprecation is always good natured and to a purpose. Lest he become his own fool of pomp, Charlie is quick to dismiss his new-found celebrity. "Occasionally when I'm working I'll ask myself, 'What would Rembrandt do?'... usually a much better picture." He hesitates and takes a labored sigh. "I'm going to stop asking myself that question."

Once you see how easily he turns on himself, you can't help but wonder what his focus looks like for the rest of humanity. If El Greco's elongated shapes did, in fact, come from astigmatic eyes, what skewed perspective accounts for Bragg's renderings? "I see everything about 5 degrees off center... if it were 10 degrees, I'd be in serious trouble." But where do those strange little men come from? "Where exactly do you get your ideas, Mr. Bragg?" Is it any wonder that his silent stare and arched eyebrow make the questioner squirm so?

Bragg does after all come out of a fine tradition of squirm art. Starting in the footsteps of the early artist-engravers, Bragg has set out to weave a visual tapestry of human idiosyncrasy composed of our most personal fibers. While we recognize the finished cloth, we cannot help but mumble our disgruntled hopes for a finer cut. Where is the grace and poise and simple virtue to which we have always felt heir? Are we not of the gods? Yes, but have you seen a photo of God lately?

Bragg's photo of God. (*Sixth Day*)

M aybe people have always been fascinated by the clever insight of the keen-eyed observer. As long as man has had a history, he has also had a need to laugh it off. Given the nature of human nature, there has never been a shortage of material to work with. The centuries may recast the scene, but the players and their shortcomings remain the same... ever enchanted but ever unchanged.

At best, the relationship between a society and its wits is a delicate one. The comic personality offers a pleasing alter-hero to the standard white-knighted type with his frothy horse. Humorists lead their own little rag-tag march with a mad-dog whoop and a cloud of laughing dust. But one sharp jab at too dear a sacred cow has led to more than one accidental beheading. Many early satirists found out too late that things weren't that funny. Their trail often left them dangling over dangerous ground where a single slip might turn jest to subversion. The great ones neverthe-less kept a sure step, or at least one bag packed, and a steady eye on the nearest border.

Bragg's traditional hero with frothy horse. (*National Hero*)

The first censor. (*Ten to Twelve*)

The masses enchanted with a hanging.
(*The Idle Prentice Executed at Tyburn*
by William Hogarth)

Dürer caught with puck. (*The Cook
and his Wife*)

Daumier's *Gargantua*

Enough of them succeeded to firmly establish a satiric tradition. Indeed, history is rich with the records of ingenious wits and punsters. Perhaps it is the satirist's reward—that undeniable satisfaction in being the first person to identify all the horses' asses in the neighborhood—that makes it a popular craft. Or maybe it's just the good old-fashioned thrill of being grand master over the cheering hordes. People have inevitably gathered around to get more. Satire feels good.

And it feels best when it hits that C-major chord called the big laugh. Being inclined to correct and abjure (or as Bragg puts it, "amuse and punish"), the satirist must become wit's best friend or die a common cynic. An amused parishioner just might pause long enough to get the point. So it is that wits have prospered. So it is that tribes and societies and kingdoms have nurtured them. To let off steam. To find the horses' asses.

In art, the invention of movable type and graphic reproduction in general suddenly made satire something available to a broad audience. Chaucer's irreverent verses may well have delighted the masses, but probably never as much as did the engraved works of people like Hieronymus Bosch and Pieter Bruegel. (Even so grim a corporate player as Albrecht Dürer could not deny his youthful puck at times.) Caught foolish or just plain wild, the common man began to find an eye as well as an ear. Graphic art communicated. Unencumbered by language, the earliest engravers spoke with a forcefulness never before known.

It is not surprising to find that once set in motion, the caricaturist, *réducteur extraordinaire*, prospered and flourished. Large numbers of satirists began to doodle with colors and lines. We cannot know what delicate chemistry gave rise to the resulting creative explosion, only that social predicament and enlivened artistry once again gave us art. And—for the first time in Western history—populist art. Art from and for the people. It may not have changed things but, once again, it felt good.

As time passed, such humanist art became the province of Western peoples' more secular concerns. In eighteenth-century England the engraved image reached something of a high art form. People like William Hogarth, George Cruikshank, and Thomas Rowlandson lampooned the conventions of the English commoner and courtier. The contrasting trappings of both high and low life, the smugness of the medical and legal professions, and even the religious arrogance of the church were all exposed as being landlocked and earthbound.

The first horse's ass. *(Seventh Day)*

Nast's Roost. (*Let Us Prey* by Thomas Nast)

Mark Twain by Chick Bragg

A few years later France spawned a man named Honoré Daumier, whose popular graphics helped sustain the postrevolutionary fervor of the French republic. In his hands satire and humanism effectively conspired against France's new controlling order. His jabs were apparently sharp and potent; his *Gargantua* so enraged the government that Daumier was sentenced to six months in jail. His work gave social satire new eloquence. It would never be the same.

Given our common cultural foundations, the visual satiric tradition inevitably drifted across the Atlantic and settled into the American colonies. As the first stages of our civil war began, a young Thomas Nast stood in the December air and listened to the bitter eulogies for a man named John Brown. Nast sketched his times, broad stroked against Boss Tweed and his cronies, and is said to have made Grant's election possible. In this century those humanistic themes can be found reflected in the art of such painters as William Gropper, George Bellows, and John Sloan. They are also there in the rumpled humanism of Jack Levine. And still today they can be found in the contemporary commentary of our political satirists such as David Levine and Paul Conrad.

Certainly there is something rare and rich in the wit who can evoke a thousand thoughts in a thousand minds with the single turn of a line. But the accumulated lines would be nothing without their narrative focus. Thus, as much as Bragg draws from visualists, his point of view is also unmistakably influenced by things literary. One detects traces of George Bernard Shaw, Voltaire, and Jonathan Swift; in his blackest moments there is even a dash of Brecht hovering among those Braggian tableaux. His work is richly anecdotal, thanks in large part to the influence of Mark Twain. Indeed, if there is one element of deliberate homage in Bragg's art it is his ode to Twain. The gentle Midwesterner provides the soft edge to Charlie's humor.

Looking still. (*The Laughing Audience* by William Hogarth)

It is this melding of forms that brings out the Bragg in Charlie's art. In texture and symbol his work defies easy formularizing. Although contemporary images are sprinkled among his cast of characters, there is a distinct timelessness to many of his figures. Nymphs and princes and astronauts mingle in a collage of non-specific human stew. One senses Charlie's search for the universal; his hope that the issues which he addresses with his art, the human race's issues, will be larger than his age alone.

For if you look back at the Hogarths and Daumiers or at the Bruegels and Bosches—at humanist populist art in general—there may well be an inscrutable depth that time has made inaccessible. But there is something else. There, staring out from Daumier's shops or Hogarth's drawing rooms or Bruegel's wedding assemblies is a dark strangeness that we cannot limit with our words. Those figures brood. They live still. Is that a faint discomfort you feel from lines and colors so queerly assembled? Look again. It is the look of the artist's eye which today lurks there still. A dull dark eye that reaches across the centuries.

Daumier once said, "One must be of one's own time." But maybe where art is concerned the power of the image should be broader still. One must be of one's own time, for all times. The issues may be eternal, but can the art escape the limitations of contemporary convention? Bragg senses the dilemma. "I don't like to bring my work down with a personality. It's always best to resist the personal attack and try to portray a mentality. Only the faces really change. You turn over another rock and who knows what you'll find?"

People are always surprised at how gorgeous I am

I n many ways Charles Bragg *is* a strange amalgam of his created kingdom. If not in appearance ("People are always amazed at how gorgeous I am."), certainly in spirit. But if asked directly about his own presence in his art, Bragg is sure to balk. Such close scrutiny strikes him as oddly inappropriate. Still, who can better identify the individual players in his group-portrait suites? Is Bragg some sort of outpatient from his own *Asylum*? Or is he there after all, looking out from each of those strange little faces? "No, they're not me. Just my amusement. That's always there."

As it turns out, Charles Bragg has been amused for as long as he can remember. He was a vaudeville brat who lived the proverbial footlocker existence with show-business parents who did more struggling than succeeding. By the time he was ten, he already had a working knowledge of the stage and its players. As he looked up at the reversed images projected on the movie-house screen from his vantage point behind the curtain, he saw the picture: it was bigger than life, upside down, and backward. It is a perspective that has stayed with him ever since.

Born March 13, 1931, in St. Louis, Missouri, Bragg wasn't to know any kind of permanent home until he was a teenager. His folks traveled the Gus Sun circuit in the dying days of vaudeville and toted along Charlie and his younger sister, Joann.

The young vaudevillians—Charlie and his younger sister, Joann

Charles and his dad

Vaudeville remembered. *(Center Ring)*

The dog seemed so sincere

"We were vaudeville gypsies. And although we were tremendously poor my dad had us convinced we were doing O.K. He gave my mother gifts like the Hope Zircon." The little contingent of troupers and offspring never stayed in any one place longer than three months. They lived out of an old Buick and a silver Airstream trailer.

Those were Shirley Temple's and Jackie Cooper's twilight years, and Charlie's parents were determined to make him and his sister the next Hollywood child stars. By the time he was five, Charlie could tap-dance right along with his folks. To this day, his magic feet can stop a crowd. In fact, Bragg still carries that distinctive carny poise—if given the spotlight, he can in an instant become the consummate showman. It's understandable once you realize that as a kid if he wasn't playing with his lead soldiers in the back of the trailer Charlie was almost certain to be hanging around the brightly lit vaudeville stage. "From the beginning... I was sure I was going to be a hoofer or a juggler. I just always assumed I'd be in vaudeville. Bragg and his Birds or Igor the Wonder Eel. I would have thought of some way to get in the lights."

During the thirties, Bragg traveled across the countryside and got a big-screen view of American hard times. When show dates became scarce, his parents danced in marathons, while little Charlie watched from the grandstand. And when they found work, he saw many different road shows come and go—the freakish assortment of acts that made up the vaudeville stage. Charlie thought that what he saw and experienced was what the world was like for everyone. "I remember a contortionist called 'Kinko,' who was crammed into a valise not much larger than a briefcase. His whole act was getting himself out of and then back into a suitcase—which took him about a minute. Or 'Iron Jaw Wilson'—he was a guy who could dance buck-and-wings while dangling someone sitting in a wicker chair from his teeth."

Charlie quickly came to realize that the world is full of things that are not as they appear. When he was six, he was thrilled to meet his first movie star, Rin Tin Tin, but was less thrilled when he later learned that there were twenty Rintys riding vaudeville circuits all over the country. "The dog seemed so sincere, too." Not to be outdone, little Charlie wasted no time in getting in on the action himself. "I worked for a sleight-of-hand artist called 'The Great Jimae' when I was seven. He stuffed my pockets full of chicks and doves and then planted me in the audience. When he called me up to the stage I naturally had to swear I'd never met him before while he made birds appear from every nook and cranny on my body."

The road was a mixed blessing for Charlie. The constant travel perpetually made him the new kid in town. Not surprisingly he failed to blend quietly into the scenery. "Every three months I had to be beaten to a jelly by a new bully. And I could really take it. Each time my dad would come home all smiles and say he'd landed another job, I would be on the verge of tears because I didn't know what part of the country I was going to be beaten to a pulp in."

With the outbreak of World War II his predicament soon came to an end. Charlie's father thought he could avoid the infantry by joining the U.S.O., so he left his wife and young children in New York City and took his solo act on the battle-field circuit. Charlie can't help but be amused, remembering that the senior Bragg constantly ended up playing near enemy fire. "He and his fellow troupers were in the second wave of every invasion force . . . trying to make wounded and exhausted men laugh. New Guinea, Sicily, North Africa—you name the hot spots and he was there." When he finally rejoined the family, Bragg's father was making a slow recovery from a bout with malaria. "Sometimes he would just start shaking all over. He used to say that if he didn't tremble he wouldn't get any exercise at all."

The Braggs are in fact part of a fine line of military distinction. As a child Charlie's grandfather used to sit him on his lap and tell him stories of their ancestor General Braxton Bragg. The family remembrance is tilted more to the human than the often-told legend of the great general. "It's hard to figure out why they named a fort after him since he apparently didn't win a single battle and spent most of the Civil War in a brothel in Baltimore. He ran his campaigns by telegram."

And what about young Charlie's war effort? "Well, in 1941 there was the Big War on and it was a very strange climate for a kid to reach puberty in. There were no men around—nothing but women everywhere. I was ecstatic. But there was a war, so for my part I introduced about 25 billion sperm into a hostile environment— my fist."

As a kid in New York City in the 1940's, Bragg had other interests as well. He worked part time at the soda fountain over at Nedick's. "For every dollar that we'd take in, I'd see to it that they got half. We were partners . . . they just didn't know it."

And although he had always been a doodler, Charlie now began to discover

The Braggs at war. *(At Ease)*

As a teen

The Spirit by Will Eisner

favorite themes for his little pictures. When he tired of drawing faces along the margins of his schoolbooks, he would practice tracing *Prince Valiant* and *Terry and the Pirates* comic books. In his mind, it really didn't matter what the source of the picture was as long as it had a human shape. There is an infinite possibility in the arrangement of two eyes, a nose, and lips that Bragg has never tired of. "The variety in people and human behavior is always fascinating...never boring. Some people can really get hung up on a cloud or tree...me, I'm a city weed...I can't get out of the woods fast enough."

One of the young artist's first fascinations was a weekly comic strip known as *The Spirit*. Charlie would go down to the newsstand to buy the Sunday Philadelphia paper and then spend his day tracing the comic, frame by frame. "*The Spirit* was almost too well done to be popular. It was a masterpiece. I wanted to be Will Eisner, the guy who did it. Anyone who follows comics will tell you that *The Spirit* was one of the finest ever of that art."

Bragg (right) and his buddies

Excited by what Eisner had done, Bragg worked hard to refine his own skills, and by the time he was fourteen he figured that he was ready to make his move. With his own strip idea in hand Charlie made a front-door assault on the headquarters of the kingpin of early comics: *Superman*. What he found—the assembly-line process of a high-volume publication—was yet another myth-shattering experience. "One guy did the lettering, one guy did the ears, one guy did the trees, one guy did the villains. Here I'd labored over this strip of my own and done everything." Bragg found the most likely looking man in charge and handed him his work. "I had a hero who was sort of a drunken Wallace Beery type of cowboy. I assumed that they'd take one look at my stuff and snap it right up. Put it right in the next Sunday's papers. The guy riffled through it like it was the Yellow Pages index. I was stunned." And rejected.

But Bragg has always been able to come back from adversity. He was encouraged by his family and friends to apply to New York's High School of Music and Art. Once accepted, Charlie remembers taking the subway in from the Bronx to school at the corner of 135th Street and St. Nicholas, where it was located— right in the middle of Harlem. Even then, in the late forties, Music and Art was completely integrated. "I was never even aware of racial tension. I'd been beaten up by all races. They'd all kicked the shit out of me at one time or another so I showed no partiality to any one group."

Suddenly Bragg found himself in a community unlike any he had known before. The familiar slapstick life-style was replaced by a world devoted to the serious study of classical art and music. It would, however, take more than mere exposure to convert Charlie to anything close to seriousness. If he wasn't ditching classes, dismantling toilets, or causing his usual mischief and mayhem, it was more than likely that Bragg wasn't in the building at all. "Like everybody else, I hated schoolwork. If there was an easiest way to do something, I would find it. I'm sure I broke the peripheral-vision record for the State Regents exam. I could look at the paper on my left or right without ever moving my head. I'd always position myself between the two smartest kids with the biggest handwriting."

Bragg on Rubens

Charlie's built-in disdain for institutions didn't fail him at high school. He had a perception of the art community that was his alone. "I went there because I thought I'd get to draw naked women . . . instead all we got for models were hairy old men." Every month Arturo Toscanini came to speak at school assemblies and would bring along his protégé, Leonard Bernstein. Was Charlie impressed by the young composer? "By his hair. He had a huge mound of hair which was very striking. He was dynamic, and although it's hard to look at him now and think of him as a prodigy, I guess he was considered to be one. I never understood what he was talking about."

Charlie's study of past masters was no more orthodox. Some of his more memorable moments were spent in meticulous study of Rubens' paintings. "He had all those naked women. They were a little overweight but that was O.K. It was certainly better than nothing, which is what I was used to. In study hall I just headed straight for him. With what we are accustomed to today, that must seem tame, but back then it was really something." In fact, by this point, following his rigorous war training, Charlie had settled into his lifelong infatuation with the opposite sex. His father was working an act out of the Hudson Theater in New Jersey, which was the only remaining burlesque house anywhere near New York City. Charlie remembers the contrast between the academic and vaudeville worlds; his mind provided the synthesis point between them. "Standing backstage at a burlesque theater is quite an experience for a fourteen-year-old who has already spent considerable time browsing through Rubens' paintings. It was a real eye-opener."

In spite of his disrespectful attitude about the place, Music and Art was to have a lasting influence on Charles. Immersed as he was in that creative community, a

23

sensitive fellow couldn't help but subliminally absorb some of that culture. "Even then I remember being impressed by Pieter Bruegel. He was just so different from everyone else. Harvesters and skaters and his *Wedding Dance* in particular. Those people were very earthy and organic...from the soil. They were so robust and ribald, not debauched, just good honest lust and laughter." It was art not wholly unlike the carnival atmosphere that Charles had known on the road, not to mention Bruegel's bent for the controversial. "Classical art always tried to capture the ideal, and the human race had been flattered senseless for the last thousand years. So someone like Bruegel or Jan Steen or Franz Hals got things on more of a human level. Coupled with their humor and spirit it appealed to me even in my high-school days."

But what about such caricaturists as William Hogarth and Honoré Daumier? "I noticed just one. Daumier's *Third Class Carriage* always made an impression on me. Mostly because high art looked for noble subject matter as opposed to finding nobility in the subject matter. You could have someone do the duke of York and he looked like an absolute putz even though he was a nobleman. But Daumier could do these people in *Third Class Carriage* and they looked monumental."

The Wedding Dance in the Open Air
by Pieter Breughel

Charles Bragg has always had an undeniable lucky streak working for him. But fate's kindest favor was undoubtedly Charlie's introduction to a sweet sophomore at Music and Art—an Italian girl named Jennie Tomao. She had watched in silent amusement as Charlie and his fellow upperclass cronies provided most of the lunch-hour pranks and laughter. When Bragg finally took note and introduced himself—naturally with a one-liner—it was the beginning of a perfect match (Jennie is a landscape artist whose success has paralleled Charles'). And although the principal at Music and Art called her into the office to warn her against mingling with Bragg's type, she and Charlie eloped six months after they met. It was December 17, 1949. He was eighteen. She was sixteen. "Jennie's parents didn't have much say in it. I think they were surprised because they couldn't figure out why anyone with her own room would want to leave home. We just took off. And her aunts and uncles who made up half the population of the Bronx went out looking for me. Fortunately they didn't know where I was so there was a little cooling-off period." Jennie's mother still lives in the same house today; it stands in the shadow of Yankee Stadium. "Seeing the Godfather movies thirty years later, I'm just thankful she's not a Corleone."

Consequently, Charles and Jennie thought it was time to move on. On the day Charlie graduated from high school, the Bragg clan threw out the stability of home life and again hit the road. Bragg's father had always talked about going to Hollywood, that bit of glamour and tinsel over the Rockies where vaudevillians could become screen stars. It had always been the next place that the family was heading, and now they were finally going to get there. Bragg senior thought that their newest trouper, Jennie, would make a perfect addition to their act—as a ventriloquist. When first introduced by Charlie the shy little girl said hello without moving her lips. She was a natural.

But, as with other attempts to get West, their route was to be somewhat indirect. Bragg's mother was pregnant and they stopped in Detroit so she could deliver Charlie's younger brother. The days stretched out to weeks and then months. For Bragg, it was to be a five-year stopover; for his father—well, he's still in Detroit today. "And he's still talking about heading to Hollywood."

Marooned in a new town, Charlie had no choice but to take on odd jobs. He sold

Charlie and Jennie, about 1950

Charles and Jennie, thirty years later

encyclopedias door-to-door. He decorated cakes. He drove a cab. He drove a truck. He was getting nowhere. Three years later all he had to show for his efforts was the addition of his two children, Chick and Georgia. He knew he was dissatisfied but was unsure of where to turn or what to do. His job at Chevrolet Gear and Axle was the final blow.

"I had to stand at the assembly line and hit the passing axles with a rubber hammer to see if anything fell off. If it did, I was supposed to put an X on it with a piece of chalk. I got so I felt a bit like Lionel Hampton . . . I could play tunes on the damn things. My one piece of chalk lasted six months."

Although the work at the factory was maddeningly monotonous, it was also something of a revelation for Charlie. Never before had he been confronted by the conditions of uneducated people such as those at Chevrolet. Jennie made Bragg and his co-workers lavish Italian lunches, for which he became something of a local folk hero, and what he heard and learned in those noontime bull sessions has stayed with him long afterward. "I'm sure some of those guys are still there." That brief glimpse of the working-class perspective can be seen reflected in his populist sensibility. "I'd never seen anything like that place. After a while the constant din alone would make you crazy. You'd come home and scream 'Hello dear' at the top of your lungs." He knew he had to find something else.

"Something else" turned out to be familiar ground. Pulling one-liners out of a joke book and making up simple chalk sketches to go with them, Charlie used his nights to work up an act he called "Pictures and Patter." His stage name was Jerry Quinn. Since vaudeville had died most of the old acts were forced to travel a new circuit of Moose and Elk lodges. But after his experience as a working stiff, Charlie figured that show-biz, even in its most primitive state, looked enticing. So with chalk and gags in hand, Bragg set out to hit the lodge brethren's funnybone; his comedy debut was in 1952 on New Year's Eve in London, Ontario. The house was full of drunken lumberjacks with no identifiable sense of humor.

As painful and terrifying as performing was, Bragg couldn't deny that he loved being back in the spotlight. Ignoring his act's shortcomings, he started to moonlight from his job at Chevy. Before long he found an agent and the agent found Charlie something of a tour. He quit Chevrolet and decided to go full force after the beer-hall glitter. "I think there were going to be four cities. Garden spots like

Jerry Quinn

Birmingham and Biloxi." He never made it to Biloxi, however, because of a little town in Alabama. "Phenix City. I was bad and dumb and scared. It was August and about 117 degrees in this club called Chad's Place, which was half-full of drunken paratroopers from Fort Benning. The maitre d' looked like one of the woods people from *Deliverance*. I was supposed to follow an act, called Tomba and Tieda, in which this guy in a gorilla suit and this white slave girl danced to *Bolero*. When those goons started screaming 'Kill Tomba' and 'Rape Tieda' I was able to do some rather profound reflecting on what the hell I was doing there." Bragg quit and took the next bus home.

The business tycoon. *(Mort Meculeh)*

Failed as a stand-up comedian, Charlie still had to find an income. Being right there in Motor City, and given his hustler's instincts, maybe it was inevitable that he would try car sales. The results were remarkable. In his hands, three phones and an empty lot quickly became the hottest auto franchise in Detroit. He traded with each of the Big Three manufacturers and broke sales records monthly. At twenty-three, Bragg was a rising business tycoon. But something was missing.

Bragg filled the void with something he had used before—those little pictures from his stand-up routine and all those drawings he had labored over as a child came back to mind once again. "I started reading about art. I started haunting the museum. I'd go every day—sometimes just to study one painting. And for the first time in a long time I really got excited about something." As Bragg sat in his office during one of Detroit's legendary snowstorms, he stared out at the mounds of snow that were his frozen inventory. Business in car sales was nonexistent. "I didn't know whether to go public or bankrupt." His mind began to wander in that fanciful way that had always been a constant to Charlie. "I started to dream about being an artist."

Once set in motion with an idea that really appeals to him, Charles Bragg is not one to retreat. Detroit didn't seem all that special sitting under three feet of January snow. So in a matter of weeks, Charlie sold the business to his partners and closed up his affairs in Michigan. With his slender profits and a brand new Cadillac, Charlie, Jennie, and their two kids hit the road once again. This time he was determined to finally reach that gold coast he had heard about all his life. "All we knew was that we were going to give art a try." It was to be the beginning of twelve very tough years.

Financial symbiosis. *(Greed)*

27

With nothing more than desire, the Braggs set up an art studio in Los Angeles. Bragg, as always, had a plan. His art history told him that art thrives on patronage and it seemed that L.A.'s biggest pool of potential patrons clustered around the west side's lush Hills of Beverly. They were people who could and, hopefully, would buy paintings; they were people Charlie had noticed before. "I have this magnetic field around me that gravitates toward wealth. I always seem to end up on the Rodeo Drives of the world." Bragg does seem to be in a state of symbiotic balance with money, maybe because accumulation of wealth has never been one of his goals. In fact, no matter what his financial circumstances, Charlie has always carried on business as if the uncertain cash flow didn't matter. "Even when the electricity was turned off in the house, I was dining in the same places as I do today. And no matter how poor we were, I always overtipped. I wanted to be loved and I was willing to pay for it. I guess things haven't really changed much... except that now the lights are still on at the house."

The lights weren't always on for the Braggs of twenty-five years ago. The family of four struggled to keep things going. They painted anything for which there seemed to be a market. "I was the Earl Scheib of canvas. I would paint a picture... any picture... landscape, still life, portrait, or anything... for $49.95." And because most people wanted portraits, he and Jennie began to specialize in them. "It seems like we spent more time convincing a mother or grandparent that their kid really did look like that than we did painting. We followed the Gainsborough technique. For the first three sittings he'd ignore his subject and just paint the ideal image, then he'd work backward until the portrait finally looked something like the client."

Business was never great but it was at least steady. The clientele was satisfied enough to recommend the Braggs to their friends, who in turn sent theirs. It quickly was apparent that the real interest in art for the Bentley-and-Rolls set was to try their own hand at it. The Braggs started running classes out of a studio in the low-rent section of Beverly Hills. "Jennie and I would have to go home at night and study what it was we'd be teaching the next day because neither of us remembered all that much from high school. People just loved taking art lessons. They'd come in and tie their poodles to the easels and drape their mink coats over chairs covered with oil paint and never mind a bit."

Charles as the professor

They would even send their kids in for special Saturday-morning lessons. Charles played the professor and counseled everybody on technique, but he refused to brush a stroke on any student's painting. Sweet Jennie, on the other hand, ended up finishing everything for everybody. And what does he tell young students who approach him today? "Quite honestly, I'm at a loss for words. I don't know what to tell them because I really don't know how my career happened—except for being obstinate and absolutely blind to my own shortcomings when I first started."

Charlie may have been unwilling to paint for his students, but he was finding more time to paint for himself. Unsure of theme or specific style, Bragg experimented in the hope of attracting an audience for his work. "I didn't know it at the time, but I was building up momentum." Most of the momentum was expended in a quaint little studio he shared with two other artists noteworthy more for their "look" than for their artistic success. "One of the guys had black hair, one blue eye, one brown eye, a red moustache, and a gray beard. The other guy was a dead ringer for Renoir."

The old guy played chess.

Producing art often took second priority to the trio's other concerns. "The old guy played chess, and to him chess was war. So we'd play war games for six hours and then paint for forty-five minutes. I came to the conclusion that you couldn't earn a living painting. I figured I would end up being the world's largest collector of my own work."

But Bragg continued to plow ahead, learning more about his craft and refining his rapidly developing personal style. He tried not to think about how bleak things really seemed. "We were living life in the tow-away zone. Things were terrible. We were still just kids stumbling along on our own, not knowing what it was we were trying to do." But the worse his personal predicament might become, the more Charlie would turn it upside down and shake the laughter out of it. "I never lost my sense of humor. Things never stopped being funny."

In fact, the only tears in his life were those found on the faces in Charlie's paintings. By this time Bragg had run into a few dealers who specialized in art-festival material and they recognized both a skilled hand and a prolific talent. "Panic made me prolific." However, they wanted work with a minimum of imaginative content. "Primarily it was to be a child, a clown, or a rabbi, with a single tear on its cheek. One tear was considered sentimental without being maudlin. Crying people were very much in vogue and because they sold I really turned them out.

Bragg's studio today

Madness in progress. *(The Asylum)*

At the 1959 Laguna Beach Festival I sold twenty-eight paintings in one month. It meant a thousand dollars, which in turn meant we could pay some overdue bills. It got so I knew how big a car-payment painting had to be. I was thrilled that the work was selling."

There were beginning to be other things that Charlie wasn't as pleased about. Although the times were full of John Kennedy's new-age optimism, Bragg began to sense impending madness. "I'd first seen it during all the McCarthy craziness in the fifties, but I really hadn't been that aware initially . . . I was too busy trying to survive." Now, in the early sixties, the Braggs' economic concerns seemed less precarious and Charlie turned his attention to more basic kinds of survival. "I remember thinking that the Cuban missile crisis was symptomatic of something very dangerous in our society . . . I found myself just walking around in a daze. The events were so out of proportion to the issue." He pauses and then smiles. "Jennie and I said, 'What the hell,' and went out and bought a bunch of stuff we'd been putting off."

It was at this point that a new distillate began to appear in some of Bragg's paintings. He is a thinker, his mind is restless, and perhaps his choice was inevitable. Even though he was beginning to make a living with his painting, he felt alienated from his work. It wasn't a reflection of what he really felt. "Most of my ethical or intellectual concerns weren't showing up in a vase of flowers or whatever else it was I thought I should be painting. What I was creating had no relationship to what I was thinking."

Being fast with his brush and palette allowed Charles to begin wearing two artistic hats. More and more he would find himself taking time out from the rent-payers and spend hours on more personal images and themes. The product was the first emergence of the droll figures and social commentary for which he was to eventually become known. But in the beginning he did them simply for personal gratification. To get them out. He wouldn't even show them to anyone. "I had very little faith in ever finding collectors for pictures that reflected what I thought or felt. I kept *The Draft Board* in my closet for six months before anyone else ever saw it."

Out of the closet. *(The Draft Board)*

But gradually some of that work did reach the public. If there is such a thing as a turning point in a career, Bragg's came about with a one-man show in the spring of 1966. Having continued to sell his festival art at a steady pace, he had by that time accumulated a large amount of his "closet" work. What he didn't realize was that he had also accumulated a sizable and enthusiastic following. "Before the show opened, I was standing around looking at the champagne and plastic cups and figuring that the evening would be just me and my paintings. You sit in your studio alone for years and just wonder if anyone is aware of you."

Apparently they were. Opening night quickly turned into a madhouse with people queuing up for twenty-minute waits just to get inside the gallery. Bragg's entire exhibit, some sixty-eight paintings and forty-five drawings, sold out within hours. Some paintings changed hands at ever-escalating prices three times during the course of the evening. Charlie tried to take it all in some semblance of stride. "I really didn't know what to think. I was stunned because that show was composed of work that I'd thought would be least acceptable to the collectors. At the time, the themes I was pursuing in those paintings were considered very subversive. They were the pieces I'd set aside for myself. The oil wasn't even dry on a lot of them."

But he learned something from that experience. He learned that there were people hungry for art that echoed their inarticulate feelings and desires and fears. "The more opinionated and individualistic and egocentric the pictures were, the

A familiar chord. *(Guthrie Dylan)*

Support the boys. *(The Recruiter)*

more people related to them. I struck this familiar chord that I thought had been unique to me alone." What was unique to Bragg was his ability to synthesize and personalize the popular sensibility. His lampoons were reassuring. Acceptance let him pursue images that had been germinating in his mind's eye all those years. "The work became more like me. I was encouraged and began to mingle rage and humor in my paintings."

Something strange happened to Charles Bragg about then. For the first time in his life he stopped laughing. Perhaps it happened the night he drove through the burning city of Watts, twenty minutes from his own house. Or maybe it was when the neighborhood kids who used to play on his Little League team began to be shipped to an Asian jungle. All he knew was that in his mind, something was seriously wrong.

Of course Bragg's amused viewpoint had always tended toward the fringe. But with Vietnam satire and humor became something else all together. They became controversial and anti-American. To question the status quo was to weaken the foundation of democracy. Bragg was frightened by what he saw. "I learned that freedom is relative. When there's no crisis, the freedom is limitless...the freedom to do nothing. You can say anything you want as long as you have nothing of importance to say. The minute the stakes get high, those freedoms aren't there at all."

Illogic quickly became the fashion. "'Support the boys' meant get them maimed and killed; 'protective reaction' meant napalm villagers living in thatched huts. I learned the hard way that people will salute anything if you wrap it in a flag." Although it strained many of his friendships, Bragg began to strike out. His anger set him in motion and he began to paint with real purpose and was determined to create art that could not be ignored.

It was in this period, the mid-sixties, that some of Bragg's finest paintings were completed. He worked out his anger by putting the times and its citizenry in *The Asylum*. But for some reason that wasn't enough. Bragg was determined to get the message to a still-larger audience; painting alone couldn't do that. He found his solution in the graphic arts. "I'd always loved the etchings of the old masters but graphics had gone into limbo...very few people were working with etchings, woodcuts, or lithographs in the early sixties. I decided to try it out."

Missionary zeal

After experimenting with the new process, Bragg realized how ideally suited the etched image was for him. The same person who once loved tracing *Prince Valiant* rediscovered the grace and power that could be found in an accumulation of little lines. And rather than one painting that might hang on one wall, each plate could father a hundred prints. "I guess I've always had this missionary zeal to spread whatever it is my idea might be—to change somebody's mind about something—so graphics turned out to be the perfect medium for me. The life of the idea is in direct proportion to the time involved. I like that. With a painting I would sometimes find that I had exhausted my interest in the idea or have two or three other images I wanted to do and I'd still have two-thirds of the physical work on the canvas left."

Things were rotten. *(The Indictment)*

He worked furiously with the new medium. "I was always going to do that one piece . . . that one etching . . . that was going to save the world . . . that was going to bring evil to its knees."

He may not have brought it to its knees but he at least locked horns with it. "The political system was exposed as being something of a marked deck. Humphrey never got more than 14 percent of the vote in any primary and yet he won the nomination. Things were so rotten, so blatantly rotten, that if you had any community spirit at all you almost had to be out there on the streets."

Eloquent and funny. *(Summation)*

So that's where Bragg went. He became a spokesman for the antiwar/antiracism movement. Les Crane, an L.A. talk-show host specializing in the controversial, invited Charlie onto the air to show his work. Instead of getting a retiring nonverbal type, Crane got an eloquent and funny fellow who could speak of the frustration that a growing part of the population was feeling. He stood out. He made sense. "It was a strange and crazy time. I remember when I went to see the movie *Planet of the Apes*—in the last scene, the world came to an end . . . and everyone in the audience stood up and cheered."

The craziness came home to Charlie's own life. Some of those who heard him express his views on television returned his paintings. "They thought they were pictures of the wrong bad guys." The Pushkin Museum in Moscow bought four of his etchings. "They obviously missed the point." The F.B.I. followed him around. "Guys with flattops and no lips kept running out of gas in front of my studio and asking to use my phone." He received death threats and hate mail.

In spite of the controversy, Bragg pushed on. He had no time for the eclectic or obtuse in his art. He was too busy addressing the everyday anxiety that was

The FBI followed him around

He spoke out. *(Prosecutor)*

Kissinger's victory. *(The Victory Party)*

Coach Bragg

everywhere. From that anxiety he created a vision rich with tension between the verbal and the visual. First and foremost, Charlie is a communicator, and he wanted his art to be something that communicated. The resulting work is a collage of bitter comic truths. He drew portraits of the idiot corps—those same old masses who had enabled the corrupt to hold the power throughout history. In Bragg's mind, we, our basest selves, were the enemy; he illustrated our lunatic potential with devastating satiric accuracy.

"Ginsberg was right. I saw the best minds of my generation go mad." People could get angry about almost anything, and often did. "Joe Pyne's show once had a full hour of people screaming at people wearing beards. I once debated a John Birch Society member about closing a play because it had some nudity in it. I made my point by saying that with his logic, even Shakespeare would be banned. He responded by shrieking, 'I'm not talking about Shakespeare, I'm talking about pubic hair.'"

Charles nonetheless persisted in his protest. As he continued to demonstrate and speak out and etch, his little absurdist legions marched on. In his spare time he worked as director of the local peace center. What the government kept telling its citizens may have seemed ambiguous to some people, but to Charlie it was simple deception. When things seemed bleakest he took comfort from his favorite radical, Mark Twain. Charlie read and reread *Mark Twain Himself* and often got a little misty-eyed as he did. "Not from sadness, but because of the quality of the man."

There came finally, almost as an afterthought, the gradual dissipation of the Vietnam War. "Kissinger won the Nobel Peace Prize for prolonging the war for four years." One crisis quickly gave way to another, however, as Nixon's administration began to break apart. Bragg's work had by that point moved into somewhat gentler themes, but he couldn't deny his amusement as he watched the Watergate parade. He felt vindicated—twice vindicated, in fact, because his career was by now well established.

So much so that his peers began to notice his work, too. He received the National Society of Illustrators Gold Medal as well as honors from the Art Directors Guild in New York, and the National Academy of Arts and Letters. Today Bragg plays to an international audience whose enthusiam for his work is testimony to his universal appeal. Success eventually enabled Charlie to move from the outland areas of the San Fernando Valley into Bel Air, one of L.A.'s most exclusive neighborhoods. Did his popularity affect him? "No. Not at all. My concerns remained the same. I still managed my son's Little League team between demonstrations to overthrow the government. I never missed a game."

Indeed, if anything, recognition gave Charlie a smoother edge and clearer insight. Having come through the emotional fire storm relatively early in his career, he has a seasoned-warrior perspective on his art and life. Did he move on to new targets? "No, not really. Just the human race in general. I got so many insights into the human race in those times of crisis that the material has remained abundant. Of course you can burn out a theme, but there's always another. I guess I just love to expose manipulators. When the system becomes their property with them using it for their own ends, the people are so vulnerable. We're at their mercy."

Manipulators. *(Court of Appeals)*

You may be struck by a variety of impressions as you push into Charles Bragg's studio in Beverly Hills today. The lyric jangle of the shopkeeper's bell. The seclusion and restfulness that seem a part of the rooms. Or the expansive, elegant, and successful feel of the place. But all of these are merely a backdrop for the collected evidence of Charlie's fertile imagination. Those little men are everywhere. Across every wall, stacked on every shelf, piled all over the floor—every surface is peopled with Bragg's errant rogues and nymphs. The cumulative effect can be a touch unsettling.

Bragg comes in to work at his little shop six days a week. He arrives at ten, eats lunch at two, and works into the evening, a pattern that he follows with the kind of regularity that seems surprising from the deviant king. Little did you know that zany Charles is a hopeless creature of habit. Self-professed to be the "laziest man in a sleeping age," Bragg's daily routine is his armor against the demons of the flesh.

The deviant king. *(Eric the Short)*

For those who have marveled at his mind's tireless inventiveness, such predictability may seem inapt. But there is a need in Charles to orchestrate and play the maestro. It is there in his art, and it is there in his tendency to be unconventionally conventional. After a transient lifetime filled with strangers, he now likes knowing what and who is coming at him. Bragg gets his eggs and morning paper at the same

Playing the maestro

Bragg's view of nature

Casa Bragg

Saturday at the Braggs. *(Lust)*

little coffee shop every morning. He frequents the same two or three elegant restaurants, sometimes in an almost ritualistic cycle. And most of his adventuring takes place in his mind. "I've wanted to try skydiving for some time now—thank god Jennie won't let me go."

Although Bragg has toyed with the idea of abandoning the social frenzy of L.A. for a more pastoral life-style in Santa Barbara, those who know him well give him little chance of survival there among the racket of chattering squirrels and golf swings. His wife and children may be vegetarians ("Do you know what a thrill it is to look outside and see your son grazing?") but Charlie is definitely part of the carnivore set. He views the world of nature in much the same way as Gertrude Stein: "Redundant." Bragg gets all the fuel he needs out of the perturbations and aggravations of the human community. "To me, the real balance of nature is a flyswatter."

On the weekends, away from his studio, Bragg will most likely be found sitting in his courtside chair surveying the life-style that his art has made possible. He cannot deny that he has become something of a Bel Air bolshevik. Much of the survivor's angst has been replaced by the unmistakable earmarks of comfort. Pool, Jacuzzi, sauna, tennis court, gardens, art, and taste are an admixture of undeniable grace that creates Casa Bragg. The place has something for everyone, and occasionally it seems as if everyone imaginable has been invited to imbibe. When the scene begins to look like Charlie's etched bacchanalia magically brought to life, doesn't he fear that he might be getting a little too close to submitting to his own seven deadly sins? "Fear? More like hope. Those people don't look like they're in pain to me."

But living as he does in a large home surrounded by beautiful grounds, pursuing his professed goal of ethical decadence, some would argue that Bragg has insulated himself from the aggravations that are the source of his inspiration. "Not so. I'm not rich, I just live like I am. Every time I hear a knock at the door I'm certain that it's the real owners coming back."

Bragg unquestionably enjoys his good-life toys almost as much as he enjoys his work. And if he's not playing with something, he more than likely will be tuned into a boxing match or, his first love, baseball. (Eight of his former Little Leaguers are now in the majors.) Since he was a kid Charlie has had an uncanny knack for absorbing the myriad statistics of major league baseball. His ability to retrieve the obscure minutiae of the game never ceases to amaze his friends and fellow wagerers.

Indeed, Bragg has an unnatural obsession for the detail in things. Not in the traditional compulsive sense of squaring every corner or making sure the magazines cut a nice line, but rather in his inability not to see the parts of the whole. That sensory sponge part of his nature doesn't miss a single fine point in the collected array of things to see—Charlie sees them all. It shows up most conspicuously in his work, where the accumulation of little lines would be nothing without the meticulous care for detail. "I've always liked small. I've tended to work small, in a small format. I love those little lines. With satire it's important to scale the piece to the weight and importance of the idea. Some images are accurate and precise in one dimension, but if they were blown up, they would dissipate and become something else."

Bragg's observer's eye is also a critical one. While the single-mindedness of his own vision in no way limits his interests or tastes, he is nonetheless a tough critic. But if his sensibilities are rightly struck, there is no more enthusiastic and excited fan. Indeed, one might be surprised by the old-softy capabilities of such a black visualist. The studied aloofness of the observer should not be confused with a cold heart. More than once Bragg has found himself with tears streaming down his face when he least expected it. "I'm the kind of guy who cries when trapped watching *Benji* on a 747."

By far Charlie's favorite art form is the social graces. His emphasis on professional and personal friendships reflects his own bias for laughter. Bragg seeks out and surrounds himself with funny people: the Braggs' dinner guests have included Steve Martin, Jonathan Winters, Jack Carter, Alan Funt, and Pat McCormack—a list that reflects his broad taste in comedic points of view. Unlike some humorists at the top, Charlie is a great customer for good comedy. The echo of laughter is a constant at the family dinner table, or almost anywhere else he goes for that matter. He is capable of inspired moments of rapid-fire wit; Bragg, the visualist, can hold his own with some of the funniest of our national clowns and punsters.

There is, after all, a frozen monologue quality to many of Bragg's graphic collages. His art can often be seen as an array of one-liners that await their discovery by the first-time observer. It may start with the look of a character's face,

Batter up

The old softy

A frozen monologue. *(Psychologist)*

move to a pointed finger, leap out from a random book title. But the jokes are there. They comprise the subtext of Bragg's work. Remembering his past, one quickly realizes that Charlie may have found the best of both worlds. Without the worries of flop sweat and spotlight stomach, he now gets to perform his show in the quiet reserve of his studio. He has been able to magically freeze-frame his own brand of wit and wisdom.

World's largest spinach salad

So now sits Charles, scratching out those little figures with their wry looks some six hours every day. What exactly is he trying to do? "Just trying to make a buck, as Van Gogh used to say." But seriously? "I just love painting and drawing and being able to have the freedom to do what I want." After spending a little time with Charles, you come to realize how much he means that. Bragg doesn't feel a compulsion to be a trendsetter or a technical innovator. "I'm not an impressionist or a surrealist or a pointillist—I'm an aggravationist." Secure in his medium, he is able to simply pursue his art. To Charlie his work, so verbally attuned, so visually explainable, is best if it speaks directly. "I want things that communicate, that are not obscure, that are skillfully done, that fit together . . . that are well integrated. I think if I do that properly, the effect will transcend the immediate feeling—beyond my own hand, so to speak."

But doesn't such devotion to the popular image, the broadly understandable concept, the (dare we say) commercial art inhibit him from probing more deeply into his own well of possibilities? "Not at all . . . Andy Warhol once said that all art is commercial art. It's just that some is bad and some is good.

"Freud summed it up best. The real motivations for artists are fame, money, and recognition . . . just like everybody else. Of course there was that romantic impressionist period when the idealized image of the starving artist got so popular. The truth of it is that most of them were social-climbing survivors. Rembrandt bankrupted himself trying to drive up the price of his etchings. El Greco painted accompanied by a fourteen-piece orchestra. Monet painted chinaware. They were geniuses but that didn't stop them from earning a living. Hunger and starvation just makes for good novels and movies."

Midway through a life not wholly unlike a novel's scenario, Charles Bragg is a funny blend of the vaudeville street hustler and the successful social satirist. He may drive a Rolls-Royce, but he keeps track of the hours with a Timex. In many ways, those contrasting elements in his nature seem to assure that he will continue to have a life slightly out of sync with the mainstream. His off-center vantage point makes him perfectly positioned to play the social observer in the years ahead.

So, what does Charlie see these days? "I'm looking for more universal themes. The work is less motivated by current events now than it was a few years ago. I seem to be focusing more on the human condition in general." Although his art may have become a bit quieter, Bragg has not lost sight of his ambition. "If I could do ten or twelve memorable images during my career, I'd settle for that. I'm not going to be a Rembrandt, but I don't need to be. Prolific artists are judged by their best works. Van Gogh did thousands of pictures and you can't believe how bad some of them were. And yet when he was good, he was magnificent."

Bragg finds our current social demons to be more amorphous than those of the past decade. The monster seems to sleep. But the violence that underwrites the human drama still materializes in its own bizarre ways. How do you fight such an unknown? Is there an etching or image that can bring *that* to its knees? "I really don't know. I just keep doing my work. That's my therapy." He pauses but continues to etch while distracted in his thoughts. "Like everybody else, I guess I feel like I'm in the wrong century."

But be not deceived. Bragg is very much the contemporary. Bragg . . . the successful Bragg . . . the prolific Bragg . . . the amused Bragg . . . carries the malaise of the nonbeliever close beside him. Perhaps, as a result, his work and mission compel him more than the kid back on the streets of New York would ever have anticipated. "I don't look forward to much of an afterlife. I have a certain melancholy you don't see in a believer's face. I don't have that serenity, and I never will. It's kind of nice to know that you left some kind of mark. That at least there will be some evidence that you stirred things up a bit." As Charlie continues to work his plate, you again become aware of that collection of muted sounds you had noticed before. The cacophony of needle and symphony and traffic that you've come to realize Bragg is very much in tune with. That he is challenged by. That his imagination must confront every day. "I like troublemakers. And if they should have artistic ability . . . so much the better."

Doing what he wants. (detail from *Eighth Day*)

Fifth Day. Etching, 6 x 9″

In the Beginning There Were Mistakes, 1988. Oil, 14 x 14″

Sixth Day. Etching, 12 x 9″

The Almighty Fiend. Etching, 12 x 9″

Garden of Eden, 1985. Oil, 12 x 18″

Etching, 5 x 3″

And He Saw That It Was Good, Etching, 6 x 9″

Sixth Day,
Oil, 24 x 20
Collection
John P. Axel
Boston,
Massachuse

Midas, 1986. Oil, 16 x 16″. Collection John P. Axelrod, Boston, Massachusetts

SEVENTH DAY

Bragg on Bragg

Q: I guess a logical place to start would be with the *Creation Suite*. Where did the idea come from?

BRAGG: Well, *In the Beginning There Were Mistakes*. I mean it must have been trial and error. How else do you explain the result we have been left with? I've always been fascinated by Western religion's insistence that God is eternally preoccupied with man. He created us in his image and cares whether we're good or bad and all that. But then how do you explain Dan Quayle? Why should we care when God is obviously such a screw-up himself?

I began this suite when there were all kinds of paraphrasing of the "God is dead" movement. "God is dead: Nietzsche. Nietzsche is dead: God." There must have been a million variations. God is not dead. He's drunk. Or God is not dead. He's incompetent. Or he's a sadist. Or a practical joker. Or God is alive, but she's gay. Since life is so full of contradictions and imbalances I just began to think of God as someone with a very warped sense of humor. A fallible sort just like us. Voltaire said that God is just a comedian who we are afraid to laugh at.

Q: How about the faces? Do you remember where you found the face for *The Sixth Day?*

BRAGG: I have every *National Geographic* all the way back to about 1890 and once in a while a face like this will come along that just looks so terrific. Sometimes I'll get an idea from a face, or sometimes from a title or a phrase. Something like Dwarf Sunday or *The Almighty Fiend* just conjures an image that appeals to me. I think Shelley or Keats used the phrase *"almighty fiend,"* which just seemed so perfectly right at that particular time.

Q: Why the hourglass in *The Almighty Fiend?*

BRAGG: Because of all God's creations, time is our only real enemy. It is the Great Tenderizer. You get old. You get tired. You get slow. You get clumsy. You get stupid. I've already lasted longer than the Inca Empire. When Mozart was my age, he'd been dead for twenty years.

Q: Were the paintings in the *Creation Suite* those that you put aside and never exhibited?

BRAGG: No. These were fun and interesting. They were good-humored rather than controversial. They represent my amusement with the whole human predicament—and the original architect who was also apparently the original satirist. I mean if he really did "See that it was good" he must have been very nearsighted.

To me, the balance of nature is very strange—it's predatory, which again doesn't seem all that balanced or good, certainly not from the point of view of the organism that's being eaten. On the *Fifth Day* he created all the creatures, and with it, the food chain. There are frog-eating snakes, snake-eating birds, and so on. I'm fascinated by a species of South American frog whose only defense is to lie on its back and play dead. The result is that many of them are eaten alive. It's complete. It's symmetry. Insane symmetry.

Q: Who eats man?

BRAGG: Well, among others, disease-carrying, man-killing insects. Mark Twain wrote an essay in the 1890's during a malaria epidemic and his question was pretty logical: when God was creating the universe why in the world did he bother to create the malaria mosquito that was capable of wiping out millions of people at a shot? It seems like a dirty trick. It's part of the crazy balance of things which is part of the package we got on the *Sixth Day*.

Q: Is that a wisdom tooth lying there on the table?

BRAGG: No. I happened to have a toothache when I was working on the painting and I thought, "How could you do this to me? Why single me out?" On one side there's marijuana and on the other poison oak. A little of this, a little of that. A little pleasure, a little pain.

Q: But man is no innocent bystander. He has been known to get a little predatory himself.

BRAGG: Absolutely. The more I learn about the human race, the more I like collies. The history of human cruelty is mind-boggling. I remember finding those ads for "negroes for sale" which I used in *Robert E. Lee*. One announced a raffle in which a mulatto girl named Sara was second prize. First prize was a dark bay horse. I mean, that must have been some horse.

And of course we're not just rotten to one another either. One of the most upsetting things I've ever seen was a bullfight. I was in Madrid and remember hardly being able to get out of bed for three days afterward. There was supposed to be that moment of truth and beauty, but I didn't see it. All I saw was the most insensitive display of cruelty I'd ever seen in my life. Sometime I'm going to do an etching of Christmas morning in Madrid with a little boy getting a pair of banderillas in his stocking. Good old Santa.

Q: In your mind it's an unfair match.

BRAGG: Sure. Look at *The Age of Progress*. Man can take this wonderful creature, the dolphin, which hasn't got a shred of malice in it, and then strap a bomb on its side. Or with *The Great White Hunter* I couldn't help but think of some of our so-called sportsmen who hunt from helicopters. In Michigan my dad used to take me hunting all the time. That's what I was taught to do. But I just couldn't understand why. I don't go for the sportsman's rationale. I think it's simply the enjoyment of killing something.

At the Dodger Stadium Club they have on display this magnificent creature, a 12-foot polar bear that Walter O'Malley shot. Now if you ever saw O'Malley he couldn't have been more than 5'3" and weighed about 270 pounds. So I can just picture him sitting in his Land Rover wearing electrically powered thermal underwear with a high-power scope beaded on this gorgeous creature happily lumbering along three-quarters of a mile away.

Q: But the animals in your works aren't always just innocents either.

BRAGG: No, we're all in this together. All part of the chain and it isn't a fairy tale for any of us. I used to get a kick out of the Walt Disney movies in which all the little animals had names and died of old age. But later on, when he made his nature films—well, can you imagine Walt Disney in a screening room sitting up straight when he sees his first film of real animals and says, "Good God, those squirrels have genitals. Where's the man who filmed this? Get him in here."

I'm all for the balance of nature. It's just that I don't want there to be one more warthog than is absolutely necessary. My fascination with the whole process of life in our animal kingdom explains my interest in some of my anthropomorphic creations. It's a lot of fun to manipulate the creatures and come up with a whole new species.

Q: But man is still at an advantage.

BRAGG: Well, our cognitive powers should put us way ahead, but human history hasn't exactly been a first-rate production. Our rational, inquisitive mind is sort of

a mixed blessing. In *The Riddle* you see that in man's pursuit of solutions to the age-old philosophical questions he's managed to destroy the elements and make the question a little irrelevant. Somebody once said that only man has the intellect and curiosity to take a complicated situation and completely misunderstand it. Or certainly miss the point. The Maya culture—so rich in architecture and mathematics and science—had no wheels—except for the miniature ones that they put on their children's toys. How do you explain something like that?

Logic and reason will only take us so far. On the average, the fellow in *The Puzzle* should be very comfortable. At the time I drew him, that kind of thinking made about as much sense as the war in Vietnam.

Double-speak is just a part of the human condition—the Vietnam era showed us that. In *The Janus*, there's no way that the guy on horseback can be accused of retreating. I did that painting at a time when the English language and the United States were both being torn apart by governmental subterfuge. We had 500,000 troops in Vietnam and we were forced into a situation where we had to recapture our own embassy in Saigon. General Westmoreland declared it a wonderful victory for our side. But then everything was a victory. And so we have *The Victory Party* and *The Liberator*. The words became meaningless pawns manipulated for contrary purposes. Justice became anything done to the government's political enemies.

Q: Those are your more political pieces. You once mentioned that *The Draft Board* was one of your first works like that.

BRAGG: That's right. I did that painting when the government began changing the draft status of peace demonstrators, or "peaceniks," as Time Magazine labeled them. In return for your legitimate deferment you were expected to keep your mouth shut and have no opinions. If you started demonstrating against the war, you suddenly found yourself fighting in it. Anybody with any brains at all could tell that that was unconstitutional, but it took the legal system five years to prove their case. That was a little late for the guys who'd already paid the price with their lives. It's the kind of logic like "A lot of brave men died in this war, and you don't hear them complaining." It taught us the overwhelming power of the system. It is impassionate and self-serving in its drive to preserve itself. People served years of hard time for burning a worthless little piece of paper like the draft card. Nothing much would have happened if it had been a social-security card or a dollar bill.

But that specific freedom of expression became a dangerous thing. I know these are old issues that everyone is tired of, but I don't think we should forget.

Q: Is the system unchanged, then?

BRAGG: Well, it's calmer right now. You think you can say anything but it really depends on your degree of ineffectiveness. There are no socialists on television. There are no atheists. There are no communist radio stations. People love safe controversy and false courage. Like coming out four-square against cancer or in support of sunlight.

We have this convenient gift of amnesia about certain of the less attractive parts of our history. I read in the War College's publication that not including either of the world wars the United States has invaded 209 countries during the last sixty years. From Nicaragua to Guatemala to Vietnam to Cambodia to Mexico. History has a way of repeating itself even if you keep a close eye on things.

Q: But didn't the process vindicate itself in the end?

BRAGG: I wonder. The system worked in strange and insidious ways. The F.B.I. turned out to have devoted much of its first fifty years to harassing and emasculating any movement that they considered to be un-American. The most vocal and radical provocateurs at the early rallies were exposed as actually being undercover agents. That came as no surprise to me. No peace demonstrator who I knew was all that hot on the idea of waving the Vietcong flag or burning the American flag.

Or remember how the legal system—the prosecutorial system—worked with its indictment powers? Those were times when the indictment itself was the punishment. Just to be indicted and have to go through the agony and aggravation and expense could be enough punishment to still dissent. For example, the Chicago Seven Trial. It took no time for the jury to find them innocent after a year of incredible turmoil and incarceration. The government created the crime of conspiracy and then made any conspiracy—even the conspiracy to commit a misdemeanor like jaywalking—a felony. During critical times the system can manipulate in such subtle ways without anyone really knowing it. That's why the *Flag Factory* came about. That's not a bad or evil person, just someone totally oblivious to the issue. It was Old Glory—the grand old flag—and people trusted that government and that flag.

Everybody said afterward that it just proved that the system worked. I don't think it proved anything of the kind. To me it's an indication that the system didn't work. It was a very close call.

Q: During that time you did a piece called *The Committee of Un-Guatemalan Activities*. What was the point?

BRAGG: Well, we had had for years the committee of un-American activities. And you know I don't know what an American activity is really. What is an American activity? Mugging your neighbor? Making apple pie? But I did know that a Guatemalan activity at that time was, first of all, starving to death. So I have food there. And being illiterate was a Guatemalan activity so naturally I have some books. And of course being against the ruling class was marxist or communist activity so anything red was suspect which explains why the catsup bottle is under suspicion.

Q: Who was *Super Nothing?*

BRAGG: He came from a quote I heard during the time—somebody said that we've got to prove to the world that we're not just a big clumsy bully. But the events of that era showed that that's exactly what we were. Big and self-indulgent. We were a great big anti. We weren't really for anything. All we could offer the world as a creed or code was greed and consumption. The ravenous consumer. And I'm certainly one of them. I've been in the running for Consumer of the Year several times. But a ravenous consumer who then tries to run the rest of the world is going to come up a bit short. I guess I'm something of an isolationist . . . when you've got the world's best moat why not use it?

Q: In the seventies your themes began to change.

BRAGG: Yes, things seemed to wind down a bit. I really had nothing more to say and those who did were starting to repeat themselves. Then with Watergate everybody was getting caught. All my enemies were being sent to jail. So my way of rejoicing was to begin doing some of the lecherous things that had always been in the back of my mind. It was my way of celebrating.

Q: What lesson does Vietnam reveal to you?

BRAGG: Well, although it wasn't a religious war per se, it just points out the basic tribalistic nature that man has always had. People love to embrace a movement. We're such suckers. Traditionally man has been united and divided by his religious beliefs. There are Catholics and Protestants fighting it out in Northern

Ireland. And the Zionists and Moslems in the Middle East. And the Hindus and the Moslems in India. Most of these movements have their inherent hypocrisies. Like the preaching of poverty and all that and then the Pope wears velvet slippers that must cost at least $400. Christ couldn't get into the Vatican because he's not dressed well enough. They wouldn't let Gandhi come into St. Peter's because of the way he was dressed. Can you just imagine this frail, simple man standing there in his sheet, the spiritual leader of half the world's people, and he couldn't get an audience with the Pope.

Of course, were I going to be religious I'd be Catholic because they have such nice outfits. I guess it's ironic that I do love all the trappings of the religions. Visually the Catholic ritual and costumes are just tremendous. And I love the Jewish Old Testament look. It's such a visual downer. Fur caps and black gabardine. In the desert yet. That's why it's fading. But it'll come back. You just can't keep a good religion down.

Q: Is there any religion in your own life?

BRAGG: I think if I could have any religion be the true story I'd go with the Greeks. I just love all their bacchanalia. The gods were fallible and vengeful and petty and horny and just generally the kind of gods you'd want around. It would be a terrific thing to believe in.

Q: Some of your work seems to argue that you do.

BRAGG: Well, there is just an incredible indifference in this universe we live in. And since it seems so indifferent to pleasure and pain you might as well try to get all the pleasure you can. As long as the forces are indifferent and we aren't, you might as well choose pleasure. That's what I think is there in some of my more lecherous pieces. Just a kind of dumb-struck exuberance for life's little joys here in the devil's playground.

Q: Do you ever carry Bacchus too far?

BRAGG: There is something of a genetic thirst that runs through my family. There was a time when I think I could have outdrunk Franz Hals. Historically, Braggs either toast themselves to death at an early age or live forever. So I'm a little more temperate than maybe I once was. But my philosophy remains the same. When I did the *Seven Deadly Sins* they somehow turned out to be a lot like virtues. Not such a bad way to go after all.

Q: And the *Garden of Eros* is just an extension of your pleasure principle?

BRAGG: That's just a very phallic commentary. It's probably the most ridiculous weapon for the job to be done that has ever been. It's such a pathetic little thing that nonetheless proceeds to drive us crazy. If you're not worried about the size you're worried about how often it's used. It's really a mismatch. Someone, maybe Twain, said that Caesar could conquer nations, but one of his camp-followers could take on the whole Roman Legion in a day . . . after three minutes, Julius Caesar was finished in that category.

Q: How did you come to do your professional suites?

BRAGG: I got interested in the legal profession when the government became the chief lawbreaker. Those times showed the law to be a tremendous Circus of Justice. It always seemed a mismatch to me when you oppose the government and they have all the laws they wrote in their arsenal. And of course the legal profession generally is such an inefficient and unwieldy way to try to work out our human controversies. It's such a perfectly imperfect human thing.

And the medical profession—well, Mark Twain said that "every doctor in the world is a charlatan, except mine, who is a very wonderful man." In such a specialized society we are so helpless in these people's hands. You depend on their expertise and feel so vulnerable. So I guess when I'm in my studio on my own turf it's my way of getting revenge. They are only human. They get speeding tickets and play bad bridge but sometimes that is hard to remember when you have appendicitis.

Q: Your psychiatrist shows a little more pointedness than the others. How come?

BRAGG: It's such an imperfect art. Until there's a case of malpractice against a psychiatrist for having driven somebody crazy, then I can't really believe he can make someone sane either. If you set a leg wrong, there's no doubt about it—you limp. But what happens when you set a brain wrong?

Man is something of a hopeless expert. He has this absolutely foundationless arrogance in his own abilities and skills. But if he is so clever, how does he get himself in the fixes that he does? It's a theme I can't resist. Like in *The Arc* you see my repertory company of experts marooned once again. And it's always the general public who has to bail them out.

Q: In your major suites you tend to gather together your individual characters in something like a family reunion.

BRAGG: Yes, it's just taking the random thoughts and individual pieces and fitting them all together. To make some sort of incoherent statement on an incoherent world. It turns out to be a general statement on the human condition.

The Asylum was done in an era of such wonderful achievements as India getting the atomic bomb, which they needed very badly. Their average life expectancy is thirty-eight and they have cattle that live into their eighties.

Q: Who is *Eric the Short?*

BRAGG: I love history, and history is full of people such as Charles the Bold and Charles the Great and Charles the Bald, whom I relate to rather personally. William the Fat, William the Conqueror, Richard the Lionhearted, Richard the Chickenshit. *Eric the Short* seemed like a natural subject. Height can be one of those meaningless hangups the human race seems obsessed with. The three geniuses of our century—Stravinsky, Chaplin, and Picasso—were all 5'4". That's how I explain my bad posture.

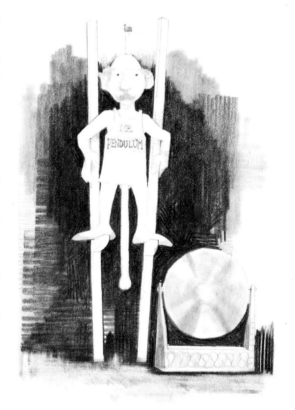

Q: You seem to like symbols in your major suites as well.

BRAGG: Yes. You can find a lot of that. The toads were a symbol of evil in Medieval art. And the crescent of Islam has been a symbol of blasphemy in the Christian world since that same era. There's a square halo for a guy from Orange County. And lots of eggs. I like the egg. It's such a pleasing shape but, unfortunately, they hatch.

Q: Have you ever tried to figure out or account for your off-center point of view?

BRAGG: No. Not really. The world is off center and we each perceive it from our egocentric point of view. It's just a strange and wondrous thing with little rhyme or reason. It's all there for the watching. Take, for instance, Father La Tour, the priest who went to the springs at Lourdes to cure his asthma and dropped dead of heart attack. It's not exactly a knee-slapper, but there is a certain ironic something that just tickles my sense of humor. Or Private Onada, the Japanese soldier who spent thirty years hiding in the jungle in Okinawa waiting for his next orders to come through on his walkie-talkie. We're all driving Hondas and Toyotas and he's still fighting the war. Or the 106-year-old man who gets mugged and killed in the streets of Philadelphia while on the way to his sister's 104th birthday party. He can make it through eight wars and every disease known to man but he couldn't get through the seventies in Philadelphia.

Q: With your *Ship of Fools*, were you thinking about Bosch?

BRAGG: I always think about Bosch. He's made such an impression on me. I'm

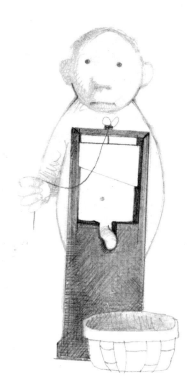

not as obscure as he is. I would like to be understood. Although actually he was using symbols that were pretty well-known at the time. I think he was thought to be rather subversive and I like that.

Q: What fascinates you so much about people like Bosch and Bruegel?

BRAGG: They deal with the human race and its weaknesses and strengths and its contradictions and its joys and nightmares. I just love all art that deals with that. Art that has no human element to it I find uninteresting. It strikes me as very sterile. Occasionally I'll see a striking picture that doesn't have that human quality, but it's usually only for a fleeting interest. I like people because they're so flawed and varied. They're always center stage. And on top of everything else, they're also clever and brave and courageous. They're just beautifully human.

So I guess that makes me sound pompous, but everything I say goes right back to me. Every time I hear myself go on like this I do a self-portrait. You don't want to forget that you're just another card-carrying member of the human race.

Q: You're not consciously trying to follow any particular tradition though?

BRAGG: No. It's just the one that suits me. I'm not trying to carry on a crusade. I don't feel like I'm part of a movement.

Q: Are there new projects or media you'd like to explore?

BRAGG: I'd like to do some sculpture while I still have the strength to flip around the clay, marble, and bronze. I'd like to do the regular crew, the whole gang in the round...I'll have to lay aside a couple of years for that.

Q: Is there anything else you'd really like to do?

BRAGG: I think everybody wants to break away from their regular tempo and do something different every once in a while. We tend to overthink so much nowadays that I'd like to do something completely mindless. Like run with the bulls at Pamplona—just let them chase my silly ass all over the city. Or visit the Cholera festival in Naples. Or go to Israel and pull up a tree in Georgie Jessel's name.

Q: Anything else?

BRAGG: Just that things can never be boring or predictable as long as there's a human race. It's guaranteed to always have lots of sparks flying. T. S. Eliot said we won't go out with a bang but with a whimper. I disagree with him 100 percent. We're gonna go out with a bang.

Asylum Earth. Etching, 10 x 12″

Don Quixote, 1989.
Bronze, 14″ high

Meyer the Flyer, 1989. Bronze, 12¼″ high

Guthrie Dylan, 1989. Bronze, 12¾″ high

Francis of Azusa, 1988. Oil, 12 x 12″.
Collection Sue and Ben King, Washington, D.C.

Glasnost, 1988. Oil, 18 x 24″. Collection Hayim Medine, New York

Commodities Market. Etching, 9 x 18"

Etching, 3 x 6"

The Riddle, 1968. Oil on wood panel, 10 x 14″. Collection Paul Addie, Reno, Nevada

Etching, 5 x 3″

Etching, 3 x 4″

Etching, 2 x 2″

Etching, 5 x 3″

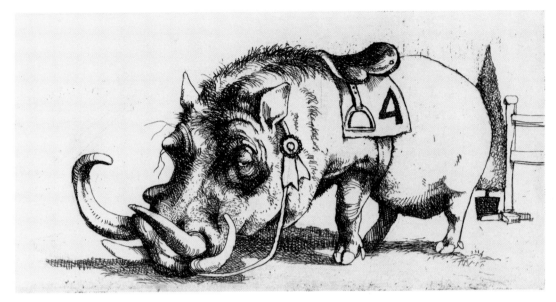

Ugly Hanover.
Etching, 2½ x 6″

Etching, 5 x 4″

Pearl. Etching, 3 x 3″

Etching, 3 x 3″

Great White Hunter. 1968. Oil, 18 x 18″. Collection Dr. Albert Solnit, Beverly Hills, California

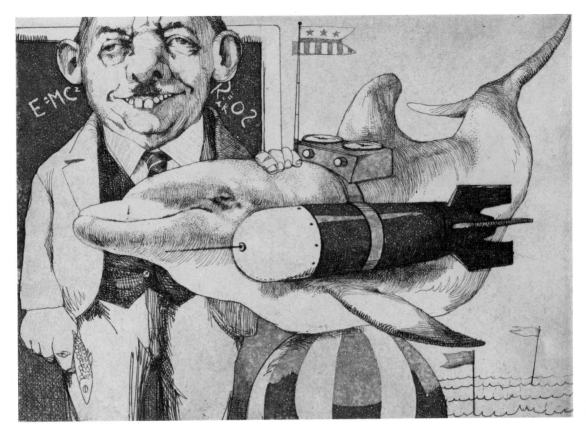

L'age du Progrés.
Etching, 5 x 7"

Etching, 5 x 7"

Owl, 1978. Oil, 6 x 6″. Collection Sid and
Judy Myers, Roslyn, New York

The Collector, 1988. Oil on panel, 8 x 11″

Otto, 1985. Oil, 6 x 8″

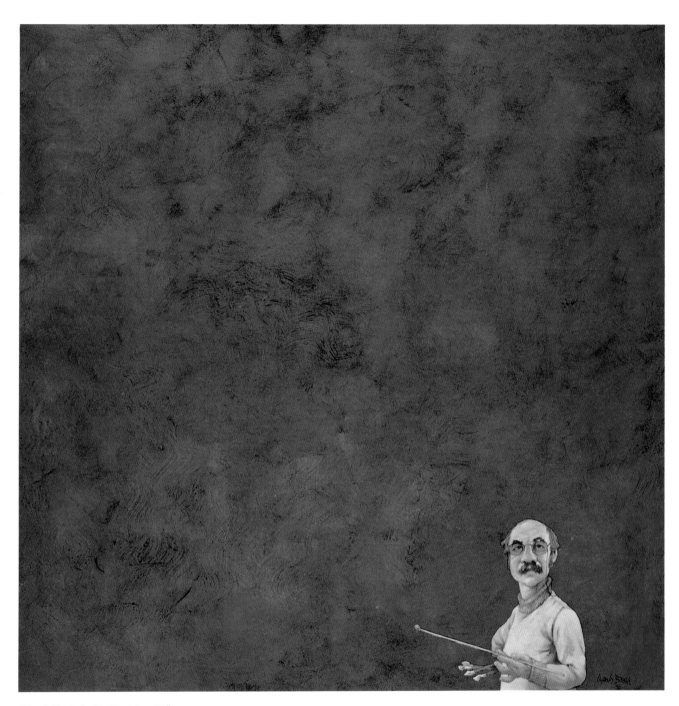

Blue! Period, 1987. 48 x 48″

Fifth Day. Etching, 6 x 12″

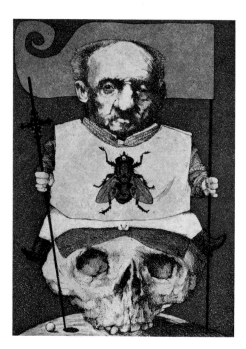

Crusader. Etching, 6 x 4½″

The Asylum. Etching, 11½ x 24″

Saint George and the Cricket. Etching, 6 x 4"

Early sketch for *The Asylum*

Lithograph, 9 x 12″. From *The Bad Girls Suite*, 1980

Chimeras, 1969.
Illustration for *Playboy*
Oil, 15 x 10″, 15 x 6″

The Victory Party. Etching, 6 x 8″

The Kaiser and the Daisy, 1967. Oil, 10 x 8″. Collection George Greer, Los Angeles

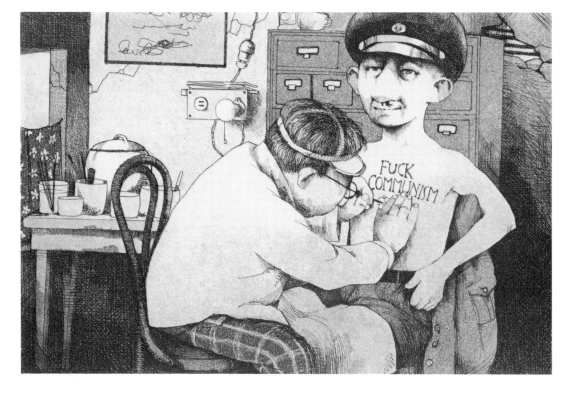

Etching, 6 x 9″

At Ease. Etching, 3½ x 6″

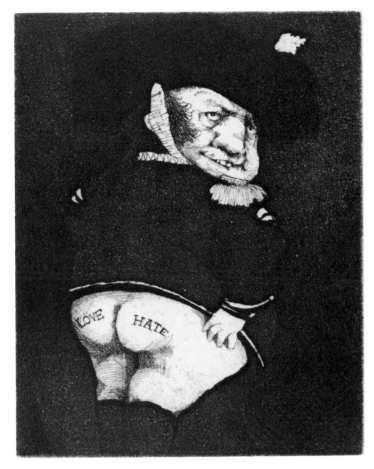

Etching, 5 x 4"

Etching, 2 x 3"

National Hero. Etching, 12 x 9"

Untitled, 1968. Oil, 16 x 10″

Indictment. Etching, 6 x 9″

The Medal. Etching, 5 x 4″

Super Nothing. Etching, 7 x 5″

Meyer. Etching, 3 x 3″

The Asylum, 1968. Oil, 30 x 40″

The Puzzle, 1974. Lithograph, 10 x 9″

THE
FORCES
OF
DEATH
and the
FORCES
OF
LIFE

Illustration for *Playboy*. Etching, 12 x 9″

The Janus, 1968. Oil, 8 x 10″

The Liberator. Oil on panel, 20 x 20″. Collection Dr. and Mrs. Alfred Bloch, Beverly Hills, California

Judgement Day, 1989.
Bronze, 11½″ high

Objection Overruled, 1989.
Bronze, 17½″ high

Court of Appeals, 1988.
Bronze,
16¼″ high

Out of Court Settlement, 1988.
Bronze, 15″ high

They Still Lead, 1968. Oil, 14 x 21″. Collection Les Crane, Los Angeles

Minute Man, 1968. Oil, 10 x 8″

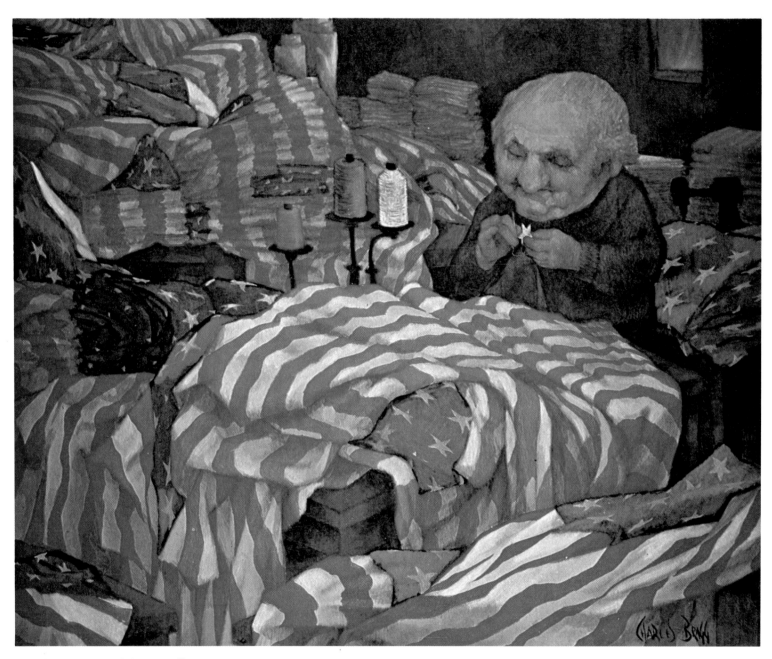

Flag Factory, 1968. Oil, 10 x 12″

The Draft Board, 1968. Oil, 16 x 20″. Collection Maurie Symonds, Long Beach, California

Committee of Un-Guatemalan Activities, 1968. Oil, 18 x 24″

Winners and Losers, 1968.
Oil, 40 x 30″. Collection
Theodore Flicker,
Beverly Hills, California

Pan, 1974. Oil, 8 x 6″
Collection Steve and Garrie
Katznelson, Los Angeles

Vanity. Etching, 6 x 9″. From *Seven Deadly Sins*

Pan. Etching, 5½ x 4½″

Bacchus. Etching, 5 x 7″

Flora. Etching, 3 x 3"

Fauna. Etching, 3 x 3"

Pandora's Box. Etching, 4½ x 5½"

Eighth Day. Etching, 9 x 12"

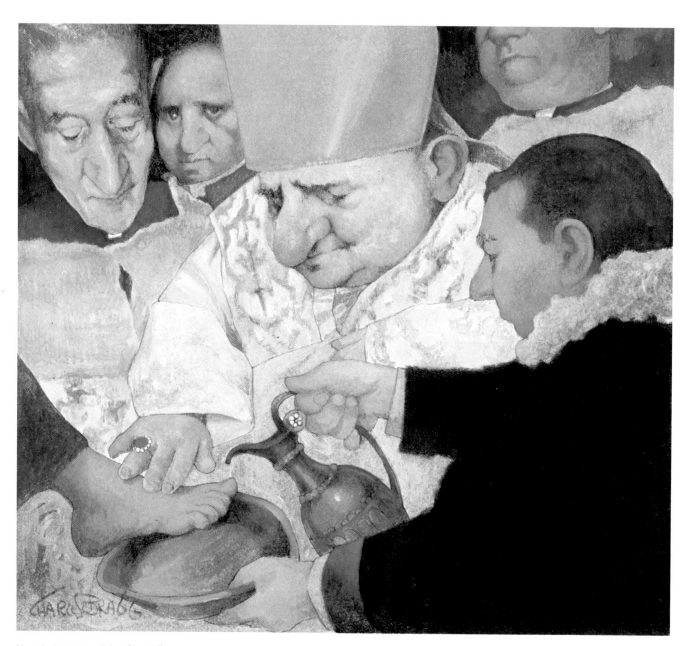

Untitled, 1978. Oil, 6½ x 7″

Untitled.
Pencil and wash,
14 x 10"

International Harvester. Lithograph, first state

Signing of the Constitution. Etching, 9 x 13¼"

The Way of the Cross, 1974. Oil on wood, 11 x 14″. Collection Roswell
Museum, Roswell, New Mexico

National Hero, 1985. Oil, 14 x 7″

Tower of Babel, 1985. Oil, 14 x 7″

Sanity Hearing. Etching, 9 x 11¾″

Anger. Etching, 6 x 8″. From *Seven Deadly Sins*

The Kiss, 1973. Oil, 10 x 11″. Collection Mr. and Mrs. Michael Beard, Los Angeles

Primate. Oil and gilt, 10 x 8″

Midas, 1989. Bronze, 17″ high

Garden of Eros, 1980.
Lithograph, 16 x 22″

Lord of Earthly Delights. Lithograph, first state

Chess Player. Etching, 8 x 10″

King of the Me's, 1972. Oil, 24 x 20″. Collection Terry Cavin, Los Angeles

Dr. Sneed. Etching, 6 x 8″

Urologist. Etching, 6 x 9″

The First X-Ray. Etching, 6 x 9″

Plastic Surgeon. Etching, 5 x 7″

Gynecologist. Etching, 5 x 7″

Psychiatrist. Etching, 5 x 7″

Researcher. Etching, 5 x 7″

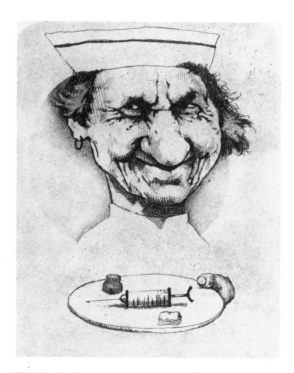

The Night Nurse. Etching, 7 x 5½″

The Filling. Etching, 7 x 5″

Orthodontist. Etching, 6 x 8″

Pediatrician. Etching, 5 x 7″

Angels of Mercy. Etching, 5 x 7″

The Gas Man. Etching, 4 x 5″

Brain Surgeon. Etching, 5 x 7″

Ophthalmologist. Etching, 6 x 9″

Pharmacist. Etching, 5 x 7″

Gynecologist. Etching, 5 x 7″

Refresher Seminar. Etching, 5 x 8″

General Practitioner. Etching, 5 x 8″

Psychologist. Etching, 6 x 8″

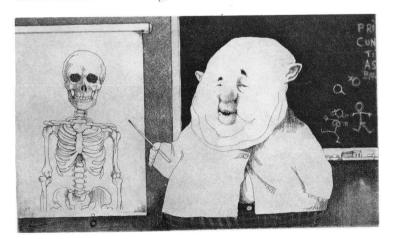

Anatomist. Etching, 8 x 10″

Cross Examination. Etching, 8 x 6″

Etching, 6 x 4½″

Police Court Judge.
Etching, 6½ x 6"

A.C.L.U. Etching, 5½ x 5½"

Objection Overruled. Etching, 5 x 5"

The Oath. Etching, 6 x 9"

Objection Sustained. Etching, 6 x 9"

Witness. Etching, 5½ x 7½"

Out of Court Settlement. Etching, 5 x 7″

Divorce Attorney. Etching, 6 x 9″

First state of lithograph for *Pharmacist*

Veterinarian. Etching, 9 x 12"

Guthrie Dylan, 1968. Oil, 8 x 10"

Untitled, 1977. Oil, 10 x 8″

Don Giovanni, 1976. Oil, 10 x 10″

Potentate & Son, 1983. Oil, 10 x 11″

Cardinals, 1984. Oil, 12 x 20″

Etching, 4 x 5″

Etching,
9 x 6″

Etching, 6 x 8″

Dennis.
Etching,
6½ x 3½″

Etching, 5 x 7″

Etching, 6 x 9″

Etching, 9 x 5″

Etching, 6 x 3″

Schopenhauer, 1975. Oil on paper, 6 x 8″. Collection Dr. and Mrs. Alfred Bloch, Beverly Hills, California

John Philip Sussman. Etching, 4 x 5″

Kid Lips Kaplan. Etching, 4 x 5″

Strum Thurmond. Etching, 5 x 4″

Sticks Willis. Etching, 4 x 5″

Art Heaven—El Greco & Toulouse Lautrec, 1989. Oil, 24 x 36″. Collection of the artist

Self-Portrait, 1975. Oil, 8 x 7½″. Collection Nelson Skalbania, Vancouver

Ship of Fools.
Plaster, 8″ high

Etching, 9 x 12″

Parade, 1980. Oil, 10 x 16". Collection Georgia Bragg and Harvey Rosenfield, Los Angeles

ate of the Union, 1987.
Oil, 29¾ x 24″

Etching, 3 x 6″

Untitled. Oil, 9 x 6″

Lithograph, 8¾ x 15¾″. From *The Bad Girls Suite*, 1980

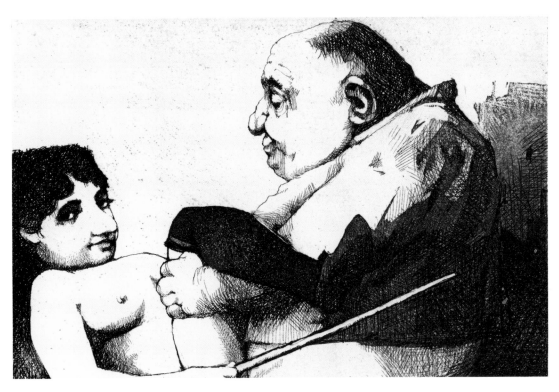

Dom. Etching, 5 x 7″

Monet, 1986. Oil, 12 x 18″. Collection John P. Axelrod, Boston, Massachusetts

Pan, 1989. Bronze, 9″ high

The Sixth Day, 1989. Bronze, 13½″ high

Belfast Tiger, 1989. Bronze, 12½″ high

By Appointment Only, 1989.
Bronze, 16½″ high

The Golfer, 1989. Bronze, 13¼″ high

Galli-Curci. Pencil

Nazimova. Pencil

Claude Monet

Claude
Monet

Merle Bragg

Alexandre Dumas

Charlie Bragg

VICTOR HUGO

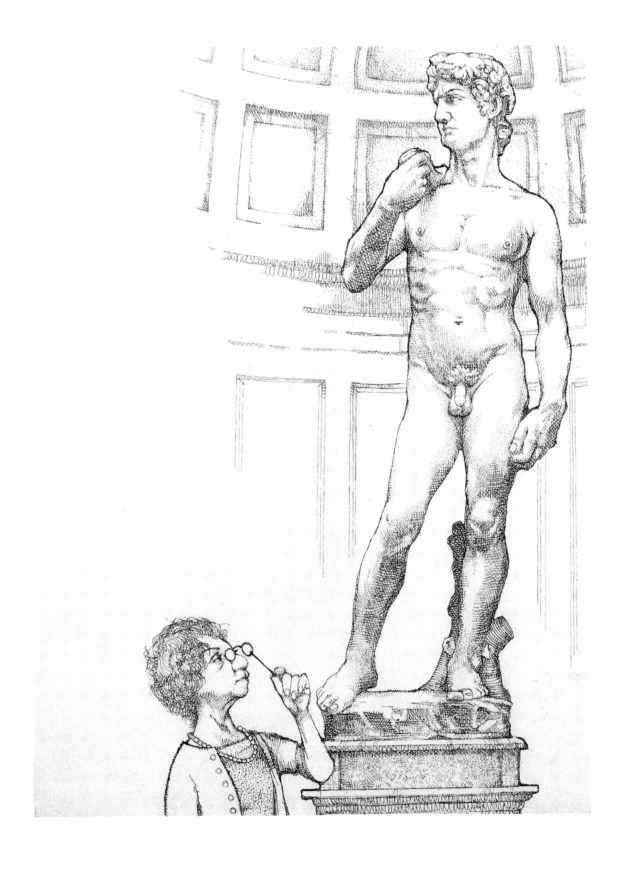

Meyerbeer

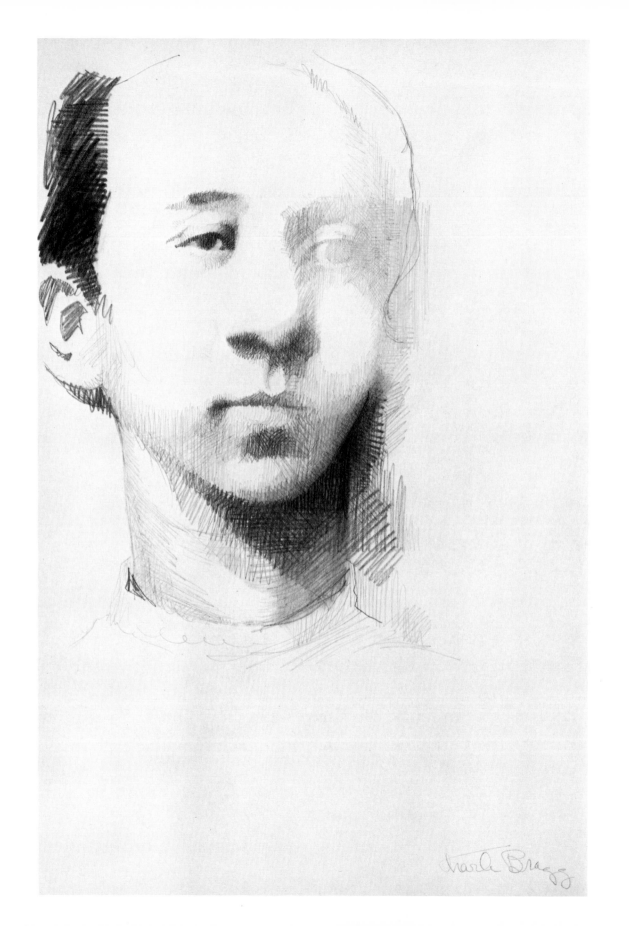

ROSSINI

Charles Bragg